THE
MAN
WHO MAKES A
DIFFERENCE

7 BIBLE STUDIES
IN EPHESIANS
FOR MEN

TONY PAYNE

SYDNEY · YOUNGSTOWN

Matthias Media
(St Matthias Press Ltd ACN 067 558 365)
Email: info@matthiasmedia.com.au
Internet: www.matthiasmedia.com.au
Please visit our website for current postal and telephone contact information.

Matthias Media (USA)
Email: sales@matthiasmedia.com
Internet: www.matthiasmedia.com
Please visit our website for current postal and telephone contact information.

ISBN 978 1 876326 30 2

Cover design and typesetting by Lankshear Design.

table of
CONTENTS

INTRODUCTION

The approach of these studies

There seems general agreement among people who know about these things that the modern man is in trouble. In the confusing, stressful, fast-paced world of the 21st century, most of the old certainties about being a man have been overturned. The workplace is changing; the culture is changing; the acceptable roles of men and women are changing. And the modern man, caught in the middle of it, apparently feels a complete failure.

What should a man be and do? What should define him? What should be the goal of his life? How should he spend his time, his money, his energy? How should he relate to women? To his kids? To other men?

When we turn to the Bible to find answers for these perplexing questions, we find something quite strange (to us at least). The Bible doesn't have a lot to say about 'men' as such. Of course, it is full of stories about particular men, and teachings that apply to men, but it doesn't spend much time discussing what is really distinctive about men (as opposed to women). What is the deep-down essence or nature of manhood? The Bible doesn't seem much interested in the question.

In fact, from its opening pages the Bible only really tells us about men as they relate to other people—as husbands, fathers, brothers, sons, neighbours, citizens, slaves, and so on. This says important things about how God made us. We are not created to be isolated individuals. We are born and live in a web of relationships of many kinds, and these relationships are of the essence of who we are. It is a very modern goal to 'to get my head together and find out who I really am', just me, alone. This is almost impossible to do, the Bible would suggest, without describing all your relationships, for they describe who you are. You are this person's husband, and that person's son, and that person's brother, and that person's master. That is who you are, and how you should understand yourself.

In fact, perhaps that is what being a man is all about: making a difference in all of our different relationships: as fathers, sons, husbands, brothers, and more. And we will need to begin with our most fundamental relationship—our relationship with God, our Creator.

One other word of explanation is necessary about these studies, regarding why they are all in Ephesians. Why not pick a variety of passages from all over the Bible to explore the different relationships men have? That would certainly be a worthwhile exercise. And even though this study focuses on Ephesians, various other passages are included along the way for cross-referencing and further study.

However, it is an important principle of Bible study that we allow God to speak and dictate the issues that are important for us to discuss. We should allow him to set the agenda, rather than immediately allowing our questions and issues to set the agenda. And so I have written 'seven Bible studies in Ephesians for men', rather than simply 'seven Bible studies for men'. The idea is to look at Ephesians, and allow that part of God's word to set the agenda of study, while particularly seeing how it applies to men in their various relationships.

These studies will not answer every question you have, or address every perplexing issue that a modern man might face. It would be foolish to think that seven short studies could do so. But my prayer is that in studying this majestic part of the Bible, and in particular its relevance to men, you will be challenged and encouraged to live for Christ, and make a difference for him in every area of your life.

The format

One of the aims of these studies is not only to encourage and strengthen Christian men by reading the Bible, but to do so in a way that is achievable—in other words, not to make the pressured lives of men more pressured by having studies that are too long and complicated, or that require extensive preparation. As a result:

- each study is designed to be completed in around 50 minutes (if you want to spend more time, there are some optional 'extension' Bible passages and questions in most studies);
- there is no set preparation or homework between each study;
- if individuals want to do some further reading in their own time, the optional extension passages can be read; there are also three short articles printed as appendices that can be read and discussed in conjunction with studies 3, 5 and 6. Also, since the studies are largely based in Ephesians, reading and reflecting on Ephesians would be a useful way to do some extra preparation.

It's also worth pointing out that while these studies have been written with small groups in mind, they are nevertheless very suitable for individual study. Use them as a supplement or alternative to your own personal Bible reading for a few weeks.

Thanks

My thanks goes to the men who trialled these studies in their small groups, and made valuable comments to improve them. My thanks too to Phil Wheeler, Deryck Howell, Russell Powell and Phillip Jensen for their input and comments.

Tony Payne

The problem with men

STUDY 1

1. Getting started

a. If your group does not know each other well, make some introductions.

b. Read through the introduction to the course together.

c. Pray that God would be with as you think and talk together; pray that he would forgive your sins and failings, and show you the truth of his word.

2. What's the problem?

This first study is about diagnosis. If, as many people assert, there is something wrong with men these days—if men are confused and struggling and under pressure—what is the root cause?

a. What do you think of the following quote? Do you agree with its basic thrust?

Early on, a young boy's spirit begins to shrivel... By the time he is a grown man, he is like a tiger raised in a zoo—prowling about, confused and numb, with huge energies untapped. He feels that there must be more, but does not know what that 'more' is. So he spends his life pretending to be happy—to himself, his friends and family...

Not to put too fine a point on it, men are a mess. The terrible effects on our marriages, our fathering abilities, our health and our leadership skills are a matter of public record. Our marriages fail, our kids hate us, we die from stress and on the way we destroy the world! (Steve Biddulph, *The New Manhood*, Finch Publishing, Sydney, 20th anniversary edition, 2010, chapter 1.)

b. What would you say are the main problems and challenges in your own life as a man?

3. What does God say?

Ephesians 2:1-3 describes the natural, everyday state of men everywhere. Read it aloud and discuss the questions that follow.

a. What are the different characteristics of this 'walk' or lifestyle?

b. How do you see these problems in society? In the life of men you know? In your own life?

c. If we are living this way, who is our leader, guide and main influence in life?

d. What are the present and future results of this way of living?

e. These verses are Paul's description of what the Ephesians were once like. Once they became Christians, do you think they were completely free from these problems (compare Ephesians 4:17-20)?

f. How is all this different from most people's diagnosis of the problem? Why is their diagnosis different?

4. Optional extra

If you have time, look up one or more of the following passages and see what further light they cast on man's basic problems.

Romans 1:18-32
Romans 3:9-20

a. What do these verses say about the basic problem of men everywhere?

b. How do I see these characteristics in action in my own life, and in modern society?

5. Pray

Conclude by praying together.

The Man who makes a difference

STUDY

2

1. Getting started

a. Pray that God would be with you as you think and talk together; pray that he would forgive your sins and failings, and show you the truth of his word.

b. A quick recap.

2. What is God's remedy?

In our first study, we looked at God's diagnosis of our basic problem in Ephesians 2:1-3. Ephesians 2:4-7 describes the extraordinary remedy God has provided. Read it aloud and discuss the questions that follow.

a. Who devised and implemented the solution to man's basic problem? How is this emphasized in the passage?

b. How did he do it?

c. What does the future hold for those who are 'in Christ'?

d. What is the current status or position of those 'in Christ'?

e. What do you think it means to be 'in Christ'? (Read Ephesians 1:3-14, if you have time, for several more references to being 'in Christ' or 'in him'.)

3. What is our part?

So far, we have seen how the remedy is entirely from God and on his initiative. Verses 8-10 of Ephesians 2 go on to discuss our role. Read the passage carefully.

a. What is our part in this salvation?

b. What is our response?

c. How does this fit in with God's overall purpose in saving us?

4. What does this tell us about being a man?

So far, we've studied nothing that relates particularly or specifi-cally to men. What we have seen in this study (and the last) applies to all people everywhere, regardless of sex, race or age. But without understanding this most basic facet of our existence, we cannot even begin to understand what might be specific for men to know or do. Putting it positively, if we do understand what God has done for us, and what it means for us to be 'in Christ', it will have a transforming affect on our thinking, our attitudes, our whole way of life.

a. What are the main priorities and preoccupations of your life? What do you think about and dream about most?

b. From what we have studied in Ephesians 2, how does 'the Man' make a difference to your priorities? How should being 'in Christ' affect them? What should our goals and dreams in life be about?

5. Pray

Conclude by praying together about these issues.

Friends and brothers

1. Men and friends

If the stereotypes are to be believed, Australian men go to the pub with their mates; English men go out with the lads; and American men go bowling with their buddies. But do men have any friends?

a. Do most men that you know have good friends with whom they share their joys and problems in life?

b. What about yourself? How much contact do you have with people you would call friends?

c. What things do you think often prevent men from having friends?

2. Part of the family

In our last study, we looked at how God has done everything for us through Christ, how he has saved us and given us a place in heaven. In this study, we look at one very important implication of this.

Read Ephesians 2:11-22.

a. What effect has Christ's sacrificial death had on the relationship between Jews and Gentiles?

b. Looking particularly at verses 17-20, what do all Christians now have in common?

Now read Ephesians 4:1-6.

c. What do you think is 'the calling' referred to in verses 1 and 4?

d. If we are all called to have one Father, what relation does that put us in with other Christians?

e. What does it mean to live a life worthy of this calling? Try to think of some practical examples.

f. What would be the opposite of each of these characteristics (i.e. a life **un**worthy)?

3. Brotherly love

What Paul briefly urges in chapter 4:1-3, he goes on to expound in more detail as Ephesians progresses—that Christians should love each other, in all their words and actions. This is one of the most common teachings of the New Testament.

Choose **one** of the following passages (or more than one if you have time), and note down what it says about how we should live together as brothers in Christ.

Ephesians 4:29-5:2

1 Thessalonians 4:9-12

Colossians 3:12-17

Hebrews 10:24-25

Acts 2:43-47

4. Making a difference

a. How good a brother do you think you are to other Christian men you know (e.g. in your congregation)? What difference are you making in other men's lives by your love and encouragement of them?

b. What things prevent you from doing better?

c. What positive steps can you take?

5. Further reading

To take these ideas further, read appendix A on 'Making the most of church' during the coming week.

6. Pray

Conclude by praying together about your relationships with other people. Pray that God would fill you with love for your brothers.

The selfish husband
STUDY 4

1. Are men selfish?

It has often been claimed (especially by women) that men are the selfish sex; that the typical man is self-absorbed, immature, and unable to think of anyone but himself. One joke says that the reason many men don't have a mid-life crisis is because they never get beyond adolescence.

a. Do you think men are selfish? If so, how do they tend to display it? (How do **you** tend to display it?)

b. What do you think is the hardest thing about being a husband? (NB. Feel free to venture an opinion even if you aren't a husband.)

2. Looking after your body

Ephesians 5:21-33 is the most extended teaching about husbands and wives in the New Testament. Before we have a close look at it, let's briefly note its context.

The passage on marriage is part of the second half of Paul's letter spelling out the 'lifestyle implications' of being a Christian. Now that we are 'in Christ' (see study 2) or have received God's 'calling' (see study 3), we are to think and behave in a certain way, in every aspect of our daily lives. Marriage is one part of that.

a. Read the immediate context from Ephesians 5:15-21. How do you think the section on marriage in verses 22-33 relates to the verses just before it?

b. Read Ephesians 5:22-33. Let's try to understand the parallel that is being drawn between Christ/the church and husbands/wives. First Christ/the church:

The church is Christ's _____.

Christ is the _____ of the church.

Therefore, how should the church relate to Christ?

And what does Christ do for the church?

c. Now husbands/wives.

   The wife is the husband's _____.

   The husband is the _____ of the wife.

   Therefore, how should the wife relate to the husband?

   And what should the husband do for the wife?

d. In what way does being 'selfish' and 'loving your wife' strangely end up being the same thing in this passage?

e. What do verses 28-31 say about the very nature of marriage? How is this similar or different to the way marriage is commonly viewed in our society?

3. Marriage day by day

a. In practical terms, how do you think men should nourish, feed and care for their wives:

– physically

– sexually

– emotionally

– spiritually

b. If you are married, what areas need particular attention in your own marriage?

c. Given what we have seen in this study, how is the headship or leadership of the husband expressed?

4. Pray

Conclude by praying together about the marriages of the men in the group, and for the points raised above.

The humble disciplinarian

1. The changing father

The place of the father in the modern family is anything but secure. After 30 years of feminism, what role should a father have? Can we have families without fathers? Is there any essential difference (apart from biology) between a father and a mother?

These are questions our own fathers (and their fathers before them) would have regarded with disbelief, but the 21st century father cannot avoid them.

a. What do you think is the major difference between what 'fatherhood' meant for your father's generation and what it means today?

b. Speaking generally, what is the hardest thing about being a father in your opinion?

2. The opposite of anger

So far in our study of Ephesians, we have seen how being a Christian changes all our relationships. Being a father is no exception. Ephesians 6:4 tells fathers how they should raise their children. Translated literally, the verse reads:

And fathers, do not make your children angry, but nourish (or raise) them in the discipline and warning of the Lord.

Let's look closely at the different parts of this important verse.

A. ANGER

i. Look back over what Paul has already said about anger in Ephesians 4:25-27, 31. What's wrong with making children angry?

B. WHAT TO DO INSTEAD

The 'but' in the middle of the verse indicates that, as an alternative, fathers are to nourish or raise children in the **discipline** and **warning** of the **Lord**. Rather than exasperate or infuriate their children by how they treat them, fathers are to do something positive for their kids. Let's look at the three key terms.

i. The word translated 'discipline' carries both the sense of punishment and of teaching/instruction. How do these two aspects relate together in raising children?

ii. The fact that children need to be warned or admonished says something about their nature (i.e. that they have a tendency to get it wrong at times!).

Look up Proverbs 22:15 and 29:15. How does this view of children compare with modern views of what children are like, and how they should be treated?

iii. The discipline and warning in which fathers should nourish their children has a particular goal or focus. It is the discipline and warning 'of the Lord'. Thinking back over what you've read in Ephesians so far, what do you think this means?

3. Humble authority

In Ephesians 6:4, we read of fathers who seem to have authority in their families, who are the ones to be teaching and disciplining and raising children. This is part of the longer section (from 5:22) where a number of 'authority/submission' relationships are discussed. In each of these relationships, authority is not wielded in a lordly, domineering way, but with a view to the benefit or welfare of the other person.

a. Look up Luke 22:24-27. What does Jesus say about authority? How do you think it relates to Ephesians 6:4 and fathers?

b. In what practical ways do you think fathers can humbly serve their families? What changes will you have to make (if you are a father) to live this way?

c. In what practical ways can fathers teach, discipline and warn their children, both formally and informally? Share ideas, and write down some steps for action.

4. Further reading

To take these ideas further, read appendix B on 'The lost art of fatherhood' during the coming week.

5. Pray

Conclude by praying together about fathers in the group, and for the points raised above.

The faithful worker

STUDY **6**

1. Feeling obligated

a. Think about the different facets of your life where you have 'obligations' or responsibilities or duties (such as at work). Which are the hardest to fulfil? When do you feel most tempted to avoid these obligations?

b. Discuss the following list of potential problems and struggles in the workplace. What is your experience of them? Which would you say are the most difficult for you?

- Getting on with my boss.
- Getting on with people that I supervise.
- Resisting the temptation to lie or cheat.
- Resisting the temptation to be lazy.
- Letting people know I'm a Christian, and talking about Christ.
- Juggling work and other commitments (e.g. family, church).
- Boredom or sense of purposelessness.

2. Who's the boss? *

In the last two studies we've been looking at how being 'in Christ' affects those relationships where submission and authority are involved: husbands/wives and parents/children. In Ephesians 6:5-9, the apostle Paul continues this train of thought, turning to the relationship between masters and slaves.

It's important to note two things before we look at this passage:

- The first is that the relationship between masters and slave wasn't really the same as the modern employer/employee relationship (although you may disagree, depending on what your boss is like!). The slave was a bonded servant, often as a result of bankruptcy. The level of obedience and authority involved went beyond the normal work contract of most 21st-century employees.

- The second thing to note is that slavery in the ancient world was not the same dreadful institution we associate with slave-trading in the 18th and 19th centuries. Many first century slaves entered slavery voluntarily, in order to work off debt.

  Bearing these two points in mind, let's see what we can learn from Paul's instructions.

Read Ephesians 6:5-9.

a. Under what circumstances would a slave be inclined to serve poorly or disobediently?

b. How does recognizing that Christ is his true and ever-present Master change this?

c. What motivates the Christian slave?

d. In a similar way, what might lead a master to think that he could get away with threatening his slaves or treating his slaves badly?

e. Our daily work is one area in which we often have obligations and duties which we are tempted to avoid. How does the teaching of Ephesians 6:5-9 challenge your attitudes and behaviour?

3. Optional extra study: on work

Look up the following passages and see what they say about:
- the purpose of work
- how work fits into the overall Christian life

1 Thessalonians 4:9-12

2 Thessalonians 3:6-13

1 Peter 2:11-12, 18-21

Titus 2:9-10

For more input on these and similar passages about work, read appendix C during the coming week.

4. Practical work

a. Bob is an extrovert Christian, well-known in his office for the fish stickers on his office chair, and the long conversations he has with people about Christian issues (during work time). The only problem is that he often falls behind in his work, and is not regarded as a good performer by management.

Jeff is an incognito Christian in the same office. He is a hard-worker, and highly regarded by management for his contribution and his integrity. However, Bob is the only other person in the office who knows that Jeff is a Christian.

With Bob at one end of the spectrum and Jeff at the other, where do you sit? Where should you sit?

b. Look back over the list of difficulties above (in question 1b.). Is there one that you really need to work on? What are you planning to do about it?

c. Are there some practical ways in which you could keep reminding yourself of the Lordship of Christ in your life while you're at work? Are there other Christians you could meet with, and pray for? How might prayer fit into your daily work routine?

5. Prayer

Conclude by praying about your workplaces. Pray for the non-Christians you work with. Pray for your attitude and behaviour at work, that it would be 'worthy of the calling you have received' (Eph 4:1).

God's warriors

1. Where to from here?

As we come to our final study in this series, we need to pause and take stock. We have learnt many things about what it means to be a Christian, and about how that is lived out in our different relationships day by day. We have discussed different aspects of our lives as men, and talked through the challenges that face us.

But now what? What does the future hold?

a. Where would you like to see yourself in 10 years time? In your:

   – working life?

   – family life?

   – church life?

b. What do you think are the greatest threats to your growth and success in each of these areas?

2. God's warrior

As the apostle Paul concludes his letter to the Ephesians, he leaves them under no illusions as to the challenges that lie ahead. The Christian life that he has been talking about will not be a nice, safe walk in the park. It will be a deadly battle.

Read Ephesians 6:10-20.

a. Who are the forces ranged against us?

b. At first glance, we might read this passage as being just about our personal battle with sin and ungodliness. What clues are there in the passage that the battle is being waged on a wider front?

c. Having been armed with God's armour and mighty power, what outcome should we be looking for?

d. Paul tells the Ephesians to put on the whole armour of God so that they can fight and survive in the spiritual battle that they face. Look closely at the different elements of the armour. What does each element tell us about the kinds of attacks and battles we will be facing from the devil and his forces? If these things are our weapons and armour, what will we be fighting against? What's the battle about?

Fill in the following table, discussing each point as you go.

Verse	Items of armour	What we will be fighting against	How this might happen in practice
14	truth		
14	righteousness		
15	the readiness of the gospel of peace		
16	faith		
17	salvation		
17	the Spirit		

e. Why is prayer so important in the battle? What are the key features of the prayer mentioned in verse 18?

3. Fighting on

a. The language of Ephesians 6 is very strong—devil's schemes, evil days, flaming arrows—but in our daily lives it rarely feels this dramatic. Why do you think this is?

b. The command of Ephesians 6 is to be strong, and to stand firm. Where do you think you are most likely to fall? Where are your weaknesses? And what can you do to strengthen your position?

c. Thinking more broadly than the battle of your own Christian life, what blows are you striking for the cause of God in your church and the world at large? How are you part of the battle of the gospel?

4. Prayer

Conclude by praying for each other, for the issues raised in this study, for the great cause of the gospel, and for your ongoing perseverance in Christ.

Making the
most of church

APPENDIX

It's easy for the weekly trip to church to become a joyless, hum-drum duty. We turn up, go through the motions, have a few short, polite but superficial conversations, and head for the safety of home. But deep down we know that it's not meant to be this way...

The New Testament makes it fairly clear that we go to church for a particular reason. You could almost say we go to church on a mission. You see it in places like Hebrews 10:24-25:

> *And let us consider how we may spur one another on toward love and good deeds. Let us not give up meeting together, as some are in the habit of doing, but let us encourage one another—and all the more as you see the Day approaching.*

Or in 1 Corinthians 14:26:

> *What then shall we say, brothers? When you come together, everyone has a hymn, or a word of instruction, a revelation, a tongue or an interpretation. All of these must be done for the strengthening of the church.*

The whole point of going to church is to build up other people; to strengthen and encourage them, to do something for their good. That's our mission should we choose to accept it. We go to church, not in order to get something out of it, but to put something into it.

Of course, we too will be encouraged and taught and stimulated to good deeds, and we need this encouragement to keep going in the Christian life. But the encouragement and teaching *we* receive is not really our concern. That is for others to worry about. *Our* purpose is to focus on *others*, and on what we can do for them.

This will work itself out in many ways, but here are five powerful ones.

1. Turning up for others

When the kids are complaining, the body is weary, a leisurely morning in the backyard beckons and the sermon series is on the significance of blood in Leviticus, then what person other than a stubborn religious zealot would go to church? Answer: the person who goes not for themselves but for others.

If our primary motivation for attending larger gatherings of our Christian brothers and sisters is to love and encourage them, then we will go to great lengths to turn up—at the very least because *not* turning up is such a *dis*couragement. You can't love, care for and encourage other people if you're not there.

2. Sitting with others

Having other people as our focus when we go to church will influence our behaviour in all sorts of minor ways. It will even change where we sit. Rather than treading the familiar route to 'our' pew, the one we sit in every week, with Bill and Freda on our left, and the MacEvoys in front, we will think about where we might sit that would be most helpful—next to that person over there whom I don't recognize (and who is probably a visitor); or next to John Nield over there, whom I haven't seen in church for a while; or next to the O'Donnells because I know they've been going through a really tough time with their daughter and I'd like to have a chat to them about it afterwards and pray with them.

3. Welcoming others

This is related to the last point. If our focus is on encouraging others, we will be on particular alert for those who are new in our midst. We will do whatever we can to make them feel at home in what might be a strange environment for them. We will sit next to them, explain what is going on if they look lost, share our Bible with them, introduce them to our friends afterwards. We might even invite them back to our place for lunch afterwards. If our focus is on helping this new person become a part of our church, then these sorts of things are the least we can do. It's about hospitality.

4. Listening to others

The way we listen to the sermon is also something that we do not only for ourselves but for others. An active, enthusiastic listener, who is obviously paying attention, thinking, and perhaps taking notes, is a great encouragement to any preacher. It spurs him on. It also encourages those sitting around you, just as our bored or distracted fidgeting will dampen their enthusiasm. (See more on 'listening' below.)

5. Talking with others

How many conversations at church have you heard (or participated in) that go something like this...

"So how are things?"
"Fine. And yourself?"
"Yep. No real problems."
"Good."
"Great."
"And work?"
"Not too bad. Flat out as usual. You know."
"Yeah, me too."
"So did you watch the game yesterday?"
"No, I was out. Heard we lost."
"Yeah, but it was a good match. The Saints concentrated on defence and that meant..."

Somehow, it doesn't seem right to have just been glorying in the riches of God's Word, and then to find nothing to say about it to each other. Why does this happen?

Often it is because we are just a bit inhibited about starting up such a conversation. Perhaps we are afraid of what others will think of us, or whether we will say the right thing. For the sake of others we need to learn to get past this, and to take the initiative in being an encouraging conversationalist. Here are a few practical tips to help you do so:

LEARN HOW TO LISTEN

Everyone should be quick to listen and slow to speak, advises the apostle James. In practical terms, this is the key to encouraging conversation. We need to take the time to *listen* to what the other person is saying.

Look at the person you're speaking to; turn towards them; listen carefully to what they are saying. Don't fold your arms and half-turn away from them, or lean back and cock one eyebrow! This may seem obvious, but it is remarkable how often we get simple things like this wrong.

Be interested. It's not just our posture and attitude that invites conversation; it is also our genuine interest in the other person. Ask questions; lots of questions. Ask about the person's family, their spouse, their children, their home, their work, their history, their Christian background, their reading habits, their pastimes... anything and everything. You want to find out who this person is, because you want to love them and encourage them. Resist the urge to talk immediately about yourself, which is often our first impulse. (Be prepared to talk about yourself and reveal yourself as the conversation progresses.)

Suspend judgement. It's important, in any conversation, not to make up your mind too soon about someone. Have an open mind. Ask questions. Listen carefully. Sometimes people are not at all what they appear, or what we expect.

Be patient. Good conversation usually takes time. Sometimes, an encouraging interaction with someone might stretch over four or five conversations, with real progress not taking place until the end. Encouragement is not like a commando raid. We need to be patient, and not give up on people. Sometimes, good listening means giving someone enough time to really say what they want to say.

CHANGE THE SUBJECT

Just listening well to someone can be encouraging in itself. Simply to be able to talk to someone who is interested and sympathetic is a great boost for most people.

All the same, if we want to encourage our brothers and sisters, we will at some stage have to talk about matters of spiritual importance. How can we do this? Here are some practical ideas.

Move from small talk to opinions. As a first step, talk about some current issue or event about which you can make some Christian comment. "Hey, did you read in the paper yesterday about those Siamese twins—where the mother didn't want them separated but the doctors did? What did you think about that?"

As soon as a question like this is asked, the conversation moves from the small talk into the bigger realm of ideas. The problem of the Siamese twins raises questions about the sanctity of life, the basis of ethical decisions and the rights of parents. An interesting and encouraging conversation can ensue, in which the larger questions of life, death and God figure prominently.

Talk about the Bible. A question like, "So what have you been reading in the Bible lately?" is a simple and straightforward way to open up conversation about spiritual matters. You can talk about what struck them as important or challenging; you can share what you have been reading yourself. And even if the person answers, "Well... to tell the truth, I haven't been reading the Bible much lately", you can sympathize, share your own struggles to persevere in Bible reading, and pray together to improve. Either way the result is encouragement.

Talk about the sermon. We should listen carefully to the sermon for our own edification, but it is also the first step towards encouraging others as we talk afterwards. As you listen, think about the points that would be interesting to take up in conversation. Rather than asking someone the closed question "What did you think of the sermon?", which usually elicits a short response with little potential for discussion, raise something specific: "That was a good point he made this morning about the last judgement. I've always had difficulty understanding that. How did it strike you?" or "Did you understand what he was trying to say about verse 20 this morning? Maybe I just wasn't listening, but I was completely confused."

Be ready to explain the gospel. In the course of a conversation with someone, especially someone new to the congregation, it might become apparent that the person does not really understand the Christian gospel. We need to be equipped and ready to take up this opportunity. At the very least, we might say, "You seem fairly new to all this; our church runs a special course on the basics of Christianity. Would you like to take advantage of it?". Or if the situation was right, we might say, "Has anyone ever explained to you, in simple terms, what the Christian gospel is really about? I know it was years before anyone took the trouble to tell me." And if you get the go ahead, you could explain the gospel yourself.

Conclusion

When we go to the large group we call 'church', we're not spectators. We're players. And should anyone say, "Well I'd like to get involved more but all the jobs are taken"—that's rather like a footballer saying that there is nothing to do because all the jobs for referees, linesmen, security guards, ticket collectors and ice-cream sellers have been taken. All those jobs need to be done for the game to be played. But the players are there to play.

So play.

This appendix is adapted from articles by Tony Payne, first published in the Matthias Media newsletter *Fellow Workers*.

The lost art of fatherhood

APPENDIX B

"I was constantly torn between 'doing the right thing' at work and attending late-night meetings and weekend work retreats, and my deep-seated belief that I should be spending more time with my children and wife."

So writes Daniel Petre, the former head of Microsoft Australia, who 'dropped out' of the high-flying, work-obsessed world of Microsoft in order to have time to chop fruit at his kid's preschool, and be there to talk with them when they got home from school. Some would say that this is easier to achieve if, like Petre, you are already fabulously wealthy by the age of 31 (on account of having worked 70-hour weeks for 10 years).

All the same, in his book, *Father time: making time for your children*, Petre argues that 60-hour weeks and being a good father are mutually incompatible. Child-raising guru Steve Biddulph says much the same thing. At his packed seminars on 'Raising Boys', there is an audible gasp from the assembled dads when Biddulph proclaims that it is impossible to have the necessary time with your boys if you work more than 55 hours per week.

All this is now standard fare when men get together to talk about the challenges of being a father in the modern world. In fact, if you want to make a modern father feel guilty and depressed, just play him a recording of 'Cats in the Cradle', with its heartbreaking lines about not having time to play ball, and "When you coming home, Dad?" and the awful closing verse where the grown-up son has no time or inclination to sit with his aging father just to talk. (These stanzas were read at a recent Christian men's convention—

I have never heard 3000 men go so quiet.)

However, the modern father is beset by an even more serious problem than lack of time. **He also lacks any coherent idea of what a father's job is**, of what a father ought to be. You see this when the crop of modern fathering books gets around to suggesting what a father should actually *do*, once he has conquered the difficulties of work, and managed to get home to spend time with his kids. The modern 'involved' father sounds a lot like the pre-modern involved mother. He drops his kids at school, he knows how to change a nappy, he helps with their homework. He's just *there*. He's involved. He's part of the scene.

I'm not disparaging any of these activities (I've been known to change the odd nappy myself), but I can't help noticing that in the wake of feminism, any clear notion of dad's role or place in the family seems to have evaporated. To suggest that he is the 'head' of the family is anathema. To suggest that his job is to 'bring home the bacon' is a blatant attack on the value of women in the workforce. When men and women are just 'persons', with no necessary differences, as feminism has insisted for the last 40 years, then 'mum' and 'dad' are interchangeable. Does the modern family have two mums or two dads?

What then does it really mean to 'be a dad'? What should a dad do? These are confusing questions for many men today.

When we turn to the Bible, we find some very clear and stirring answers to these puzzling questions. In the Bible, a father is much more than just 'dad', the friendly, involved nice-guy who does his share of the ironing, and turns up to watch you score the winning goal.

There are many different facets to the Bible's picture of fatherhood. Let's look at three of the most important ones, before thinking about their implications.

Basic concepts

One of the primary aspects of biblical fatherhood is that father's **generate and sustain life**. This may seem a little strange to us as modern readers. We tend to think of mothers as the ones who generate new life, with fathers as junior partners in the process, having a fairly small part to play (now easily replaceable by artificial means). In the Bible, it is almost the other way around. While the role of the mother is never downplayed, it is the fathers who do the 'begetting' in the Bible. They spawn new life. They initiate the existence of another being, who is in their likeness and image, as Adam did with Seth (Gen 5:3).

It is in much the same sense that God is the father of all mankind. As Moses says, "Is he not your father, your Creator, who made you and formed you?" (Deut 32:6), or as Malachi puts it: "Have we not all one father? Did not one God create us?" (Mal 2:10).

Fathers are the source of life to generation after generation of their descendants, like Jubal who was 'the father of those who dwell in tents and keep cattle', or most famously of Abraham, who was father to a nation, even to many nations.

A second basic concept is related to the first. In the Bible, fathers **are seen as being responsible** for the life they have initiated and brought into being. To both parents, but particularly to the father, is sheeted home the responsibility to take action for the growth of his children, to seek the welfare of his 'house' or family. In doing so, fathers imitate the faithfulness of the great Father and Creator of us all, who provides for and supervises and sustains all his creation, opening his hand to all, sending his rain on the just and unjust alike. Just as God in his goodness takes responsibility for his creation, so fathers take responsibility for their families.

The third basic concept of fatherhood is directly related to the second. The **authority** that a father possesses in the family does not come from his physical strength or dominance, nor from some arbitrary decision by God (as if God flipped a coin to see who would be the head of the family, and the wife 'lost'… or should that be 'won'?). The father has authority because he has responsibility. The buck stops with him, and so the final call also stops with him. He rules the family not in order to advance his own interests, but in order to fulfil his responsibility. It is no accident that Ephesians 5 speaks of a husband expressing his 'headship' over his wife by laying down his life for her. This is the nature of the father's authority. It is simply the flip-side of his responsibility to give of himself, to the fullest extent, for the benefit of his family.

Thus, honour and obedience are due to a father because he is the source of life, and the one who accepts responsibility for that life, to feed it, nourish it, establish it, teach it and direct it. Just as God the Father is worthy of honour and thanks because he created all things, and in his goodness takes responsibility for sustaining his creation, so human fathers are worthy of honour from their families. Modern readers can find it hard to understand the horror that the Bible expresses when sons or daughters dishonour or mock their parents. But this is because we do not appreciate the profound responsibility, and hence profound authority, that is invested in a father and mother: "The eye that mocks a father and scorns to obey a mother will be picked out by the ravens of the valley and eaten by the vultures" (Prov 30:17).

A picture of fatherhood

These three related concepts—generation, responsibility and authority—together form the basis for the many pictures and examples of fatherhood that we see in the Bible. Different aspects are emphasized at different points.

When Job says that he was a "father to the poor", he is emphasizing his compassion and care for them, how he took responsibility for them, and provided for them (Job 29:16). Likewise when Joseph says that God had made him a "father to Pharaoh", he means that his place and status in Egypt was beyond that of even Pharaoh. He had become the one they all looked to for survival, Pharaoh included, and consequently was "lord of the entire household and ruler of Egypt" (Gen 45:8). Likewise in Isaiah 22, when Eliakim is made the new steward of Jerusalem instead of Shebna, note how his role is described:

> I will clothe him [Eliakim] with your [Shebna's] robe, and will bind your girdle on him, and will commit your authority to his hand; and he shall be a father to the inhabitants of Jerusalem and to the house of Judah.

He is a 'father' in the sense that authority has now been conferred upon him, but it is an authority for the good of the people, to dispense justice and to manage the affairs of the city for the good of the city. Likewise, when the child is born in Isaiah 9, the One on whose shoulders the government will rest, who will rule over the kingdom for ever, bringing peace and justice and righteousness, what should his name be but 'everlasting father'.

When we look at 'fathers' in the Bible, a rich and stirring picture emerges. The biblical father is not a stern, authoritative figure, distant, severe, wielding his lordly power with scant regard for others. He is compassionate and righteous, an open-handed provider and sustainer, whose authority is expressed in the goodness and kindness which he shows towards those he takes responsibility for. He gives good gifts to his children, he rebukes his son because he loves him, he teaches and trains him in the way of righteousness, he exhorts and encourages. He is unquestionably in charge, but we see him exercise that leadership in goodness and positive action for the sake of others, not in lording it over his minions for his own selfish benefit. We obey him and give him honour, gladly and lavishly, because he is so worthy of it.

Am I talking about God the Father here, or human fathers? The answer is both. This description applies to God and to human fathers in the Bible. For it is ultimately from God the Father that all human fatherhood derives its name, as Ephesians 3:14 puts it. He is the one before whom we kneel, to ask that he might strengthen us from his glorious riches, that he would give us that we most need, namely Christ dwelling in our hearts. This is a beautiful picture of fatherhood—of children coming to their strong, wise, gracious father, and asking for what they need. And him granting it gladly and richly, out of his love for them.

What to do

Modern fathers need to recapture this biblical vision of fatherhood. In the confusing environment of modern gender politics and redefinition of the family, we need to regain our confidence in the imposing biblical portrait of the life-giving, responsible, ruling father.

In practical terms, this means expressing our leadership and authority in the family by taking responsibility for the family's welfare. Or to put it in reverse, to express our responsibility for the family by making decisions and taking action for its benefit.

It's not simply that we need to get home a little earlier and have time to read our children a bed-time story. That may be a starting point, but it is only one small aspect of what is required. As fathers, we need to take responsibility for the total welfare of our families—their physical, emotional and spiritual wellbeing. It is our responsibility. We are accountable. We do it in partnership with our wives, but the responsibility is ultimately ours.

If our children are hungry and poorly clothed, it is up to us to do something about it—to take whatever action is necessary to meet that need. What's more, most of us do a passable job at it, and plan our lives and priorities to make sure that these needs are met. We don't sit around watching the cricket every day, and then notice one morning that little Johnny is suffering from malnutrition and say to ourselves, "By gee, I'd better think about getting a job".

Yet when it comes to other aspects of our fatherly care, many of us are rather more neglectful and reactive. We don't spend the time we should building strong, trusting relationships with our children. We don't take the initiative to teach, instruct and talk with our children about the things of God, or to pray with them and for them. But no-one is going to do this for us, or assume responsibility for us. It is our responsibility, and we need to take decisive, thoughtful action.

Make some time to think about it. What action are you going to take, in order to be a father to your family?

This appendix is adapted from an article by Tony Payne, first published in the Matthias Media newsletter *Fellow Workers*.

Five reasons to get out
of bed on Monday morning

APPENDIX C

How do you feel when the alarm clock rings on Monday morning? Do you jump out of bed eager to start another working week? Not likely! Many of us spend 40, 50, 60+ hours a week at work. I am thinking of both paid and unpaid work, work at home and away from home. That's about half of our waking hours, especially if you have travel time. Work is sometimes enjoyable and sometimes satisfying. But sometimes it's dead boring, sometimes it's difficult, frustrating and stressful—definitely a health hazard!—and other times it's so mundane, so insignificant. When I left school I was employed as a 'gofer' (a person who 'goes for' things) on a building site. My main job was to test concrete. After each pour I placed a sample in a steel cylinder. I had to fill it in 3 layers and prod each layer 25 times with a steel bar. It was so boring. It seemed so mundane. I thought I was going to go crazy! I was glad it only lasted 2 months.

Do you ever ask why you work? What is your attitude to your daily work?

Is work simply an evil necessity? We have to work to put the food on the table, to put a roof over our head and to pay the bills. It's something we have to endure to survive. "I owe. I owe it's off to work I go." I don't want to go to work but I have to.

Is work part of the curse on the human race because of our rebellion against God?

And being a Christian doesn't necessarily make it any easier. It can make it harder. This comes about because of the Sunday-Monday crunch. On Sunday our minds are filled with the work of God. As we read the Bible we see that God is doing a great eternal work. He is sending out the great news about Jesus and drawing rebels into his kingdom. He is making sinners holy. Then on Monday we change gears with an almighty crunch. We go back to prodding the concrete or the endless paperwork which seems so insignificant, so temporary, so ordinary compared to what God is doing.

We may find that the more we're involved in Christian work the more frustrating our day-to-day work is. In Christian work we see people brought from Hell to Heaven. In comparison, prodding concrete seems so mundane. We can begin to feel second rate. It seems that the really important people in God's economy are those who are preaching the gospel full-time. They are involved in the eternal work. Concrete test samples will pass away. Is non-gospel work second rate? More thoughts on this in a moment...

So why work? What is God's wisdom on this activity that takes up so much of our time? What do the Scriptures have to say to us about our day to day work? I found five reasons in the New Testament for why the Christian works.

1. So as not to burden others

Paul worked hard in Thessalonica at both preaching and tent making. Why? It was out of concern for the Thessalonians—so that he wouldn't be a burden on any of them as he brought the gospel to them. (2 Thess 3:7-8). He told them to follow his example. "If a man will not work, he shall not eat"(v. 10). Each Christian should work so as not to burden others. Note that Paul is talking about those who can work but will not, not those who want to work but who cannot find work or are not able to work. The genuinely unemployed deserve compassion and help not condemnation.

Paul had said a similar thing in 1 Thessalonians: "Make it your ambition to lead a quiet life, to mind your own business and to work with your hands, just as we told you, so that your daily life may win the respect of outsiders and so that you will not be dependent on anybody" (4:11, 12). Notice here a further reason—to win the respect of outsiders. We do not live our lives in a vacuum. The non-Christian world is watching us. If we are lazy and bludge off others, then people will draw their conclusions about Christianity. If we work hard and provide for ourselves, we bring credit to Christ. We are to work to win the respect of the watching world.

I mentioned earlier the Sun-Mon crunch and how as believers our day-to-day work can seem second rate compared with gospel work. But this verse shows the fallacy in that sort of thinking. We all are involved in the spread of the gospel. The way we live our lives either hinders or helps the spread of the gospel. And part of that is our attitude to work. If we are lazy and sponge off others then we hinder the gospel. If we work hard and provide for ourselves then we help the spread of the gospel.

And notice the context. Verses 9 and 10 are about love for fellow believers. Verse 11 begins a new paragraph in the NIV, but in the original the thought carries on. Paul is still talking about love. We work out of love for others. As we've seen already, we love others by working so we won't burden them and so win respect for Christ. We work because it's loving to work. Love is the fruit of the gospel. And part of love for others is work.

2. To serve the community

Let us not become weary in doing good, for at the proper time we will reap a harvest if we do not give up. Therefore, as we have opportunity, let us do good to all people, especially to those who belong to the family of believers.

Galatians 6:9,10

As Christians we are called to do good to all people. We are to be like our heavenly Father who sends rain on the good and the bad. Hopefully we can find a job where we are doing good for people. Even that job I had prodding concrete was doing good. I was part of a team building the Flemington Markets in Sydney. I was helping to provide the community with an efficient way of getting their vegies! It was boring, but it was loving, too.

3. To provide for family and relatives

The apostle Paul wrote to Timothy, "Give proper recognition to those widows who are really in need. But if a widow has children or grandchildren, these should learn first of all to put their religion into practice by caring for their own family and so repaying their parents and grandparents, for this is pleasing to God." (1 Tim 5:3,4). It pleases God when we care for our own families and parents and grandparents. That is another good reason for working, either to directly help our relatives by caring for them ourselves or by earning money which we can use to help them. Again it's part of love. This is where most unpaid work fits in. Most unpaid work is in caring for your own family in some way. This is why we must banish from our language that terrible phrase—"I'm just a housewife". What a ludicrous phrase. It's like the nation's leader saying "I'm just the Prime Minister" or a preacher saying "I just preach the gospel". In fact, caring for families is one of the few occupations I can think of that has direct biblical warrant. The fact that it is often unpaid is irrelevant.

4. So that you've got something to share with those in need

> He who has been stealing must steal no longer, but must work, doing something useful with his own hands, that he may have something to share with those in need.
>
> Ephesians 4:28

Why work? Again, love. And again, love as the fruit of the gospel in our lives. This whole section of Ephesians (4:17-6:24) is about leaving behind the old way of life without Christ and living the new life in Christ, which is a life of love. That includes working so you can give, instead of stealing.

5. To support gospel workers

In Philippians 1:3-5, Paul speaks about the partnership in the gospel that he shared with the Philippian Christians. What was the Philippians' role in this partnership? Paul mentions one aspect later in the letter:

> *Moreover, as you Philippians know, in the early days of your acquaintance with the gospel, when I set out from Macedonia, not one church shared with me in the matter of giving and receiving, except you only; for even when I was in Thessalonica, you sent me aid again and again when I was in need.*
>
> *Philippians 4:15,16*

It was partly a financial partnership. The material help from the Philippians enabled Paul to continue preaching the gospel.

The same is true today. Our giving can free up others from their daily work so they can preach the gospel full-time or part-time. Most congregations work this way. Many members slave away 40 or 50 hours a week to earn money and then give some away to free up others from daily work so they can preach the gospel. Overseas missionaries are supported in the same way.

This is also helpful in overcoming the Sun-Mon crunch and the feeling that non-gospel work is second rate. The gospel workers and the other workers are in a partnership. They are working together for the spread of the gospel. They have different roles but the same goal. It's not a matter of first rate and second rate— one being secular and one holy—both are working together in the holy work of spreading the gospel. What a great reason to work! To free others for gospel work. No way is that second rate!

There are five very good reasons to go to work next Monday morning: Because it's a loving thing not to burden others, and so win respect for Christ. Because it's a loving thing to serve the community and to provide for your family. Because it's a loving thing to work so you can give to the needy and so you can give to gospel work.

None of this denies the fact that work is difficult. And work is difficult because of the curse of God on our rebellion. But that doesn't mean that work itself is part of the curse. Adam worked in the Garden before the curse. Work is difficult and frustrating and painful because we live in a fallen world, but it is not evil. Work is good if it is done in love. It's a good thing to spend half your waking hours doing. It should be done as part of our response to God's amazing love for us. It's part of the fruit of the gospel in our lives. It would be nice to be sailing seven days a week. But would it be loving?

I want a new bumper sticker: not "I owe, I owe, it's off to work I go", but "I love, I love, it's off to work I shove".

Do you think it could catch on?

Feedback on this resource

We really appreciate getting feedback about our resources—not just suggestions for how to improve them, but also positive feedback and ways they can be used. We especially love to hear that the resources may have helped someone in their Christian growth.

You can send feedback to us via the 'Feedback' menu in our online store, or write to us at info@matthiasmedia.com.au.

This appendix is adapted from an article by James Davidson, first published in *The Briefing*.

matthiasmedia

Matthias Media is an evangelical publishing ministry that seeks to persuade all Christians of the truth of God's purposes in Jesus Christ as revealed in the Bible, and equip them with high-quality resources, so that by the work of the Holy Spirit they will:

- abandon their lives to the honour and service of Christ in daily holiness and decision-making
- pray constantly in Christ's name for the fruitfulness and growth of his gospel
- speak the Bible's life-changing word whenever and however they can—in the home, in the world and in the fellowship of his people.

Our resources range from Bible studies and books through to training courses, audio sermons and children's Sunday School material. To find out more, and to access samples and free downloads, visit our website:

www.matthiasmedia.com

How to buy our resources

1. Direct from us over the internet:
   – in the US: www.matthiasmedia.com
   – in Australia: www.matthiasmedia.com.au

2. Direct from us by phone: please visit our website for current phone contact information.

3. Through a range of outlets in various parts of the world. Visit **www.matthiasmedia.com/contact** for details about recommended retailers in your part of the world.

4. Trade enquiries can be addressed to:
   – in the US and Canada: sales@matthiasmedia.com
   – in Australia and the rest of the world: sales@matthiasmedia.com.au

Register at our website for our **free** regular email update to receive information about the latest new resources, **exclusive special offers**, and free articles to help you grow in your Christian life and ministry.

Other Interactive and Topical Bible Studies from Matthias Media

Our Interactive Bible Studies (IBS) and Topical Bible Studies (TBS) are a valuable resource to help you keep feeding from God's word. The IBS series works through passages and books of the Bible; the TBS series pulls together the Bible's teaching on topics such as money or prayer. As of July 2018, the series contains the following titles:

Beyond Eden
GENESIS 1-11
Authors: Phillip Jensen and Tony Payne, 9 studies

Out of Darkness
EXODUS 1-18
Author: Andrew Reid, 8 studies

The Shadow of Glory
EXODUS 19-40
Author: Andrew Reid, 7 studies

The One and Only
DEUTERONOMY
Author: Bryson Smith, 8 studies

Remember the Rock
JOSHUA
Author: Phil Campbell, 6 studies

The Good, the Bad and the Ugly
JUDGES
Author: Mark Baddeley, 10 studies

Famine and Fortune
RUTH
Authors: Barry Webb and David Höhne, 4 studies

God Will Have His King
1 SAMUEL
Author: Des Smith, 9 studies

Renovator's Dream
NEHEMIAH
Authors: Phil Campbell and Greg Clarke, 7 studies

The Eye of the Storm
JOB
Author: Bryson Smith, 6 studies

The Beginning of Wisdom
PROVERBS VOLUME 1
Author: Joshua Ng, 7 studies

Living the Good Life
PROVERBS VOLUME 2
Author: Joshua Ng, 8 studies

The Search for Meaning
ECCLESIASTES
Author: Tim McMahon, 9 studies

Garden of Love
SONG OF SONGS
Author: Des Smith, 4 studies

Two Cities
ISAIAH
Authors: Andrew Reid and Karen Morris, 9 studies

Kingdom of Dreams
DANIEL
Authors: Andrew Reid and Karen Morris, 9 studies

Burning Desire
OBADIAH AND MALACHI
Authors: Phillip Jensen and Richard Pulley, 6 studies

Warning Signs
JONAH
Author: Andrew Reid, 6 studies

Living by Faith
HABAKKUK
Author: Ian Carmichael, 5 studies

On That Day
ZECHARIAH
Author: Tim McMahon, 8 studies

Full of Promise
THE BIG PICTURE OF THE O.T.
Authors: Phil Campbell and Bryson Smith, 8 studies

The Good Living Guide
MATTHEW 5:1-12
Authors: Phillip Jensen and Tony Payne, 9 studies

News of the Hour
MARK
Authors: Peter Bolt and Tony Payne, 10 studies

Proclaiming the Risen Lord
LUKE 24-ACTS 2
Author: Peter Bolt, 6 studies

Mission Unstoppable
ACTS
Author: Bryson Smith, 10 studies

The Free Gift of Life
ROMANS 1-5
Author: Gordon Cheng, 8 studies

The Free Gift of Sonship
ROMANS 6-11
Author: Gordon Cheng, 8 studies

The Freedom of Christian Living
ROMANS 12-16
Author: Gordon Cheng, 7 studies

Free for All
GALATIANS
Authors: Phillip Jensen and Kel Richards, 8 studies

Walk this Way
EPHESIANS
Author: Bryson Smith, 8 studies

Partners for Life
PHILIPPIANS
Author: Tim Thorburn, 8 studies

The Complete Christian
COLOSSIANS
Authors: Phillip Jensen and Tony Payne, 8 studies

To the Householder
1 TIMOTHY
Authors: Phillip Jensen and Greg Clarke, 9 studies

Run the Race
2 TIMOTHY
Author: Bryson Smith, 6 studies

The Path to Godliness
TITUS
Authors: Phillip Jensen and Tony Payne, 7 studies

From Shadow to Reality
HEBREWS
Author: Joshua Ng, 10 studies

The Implanted Word
JAMES
Authors: Phillip Jensen and Kirsten Birkett, 8 studies

Homeward Bound
1 PETER
Authors: Phillip Jensen and Tony Payne, 10 studies

All You Need to Know
2 PETER
Author: Bryson Smith, 6 studies

Rest Assured
1 JOHN
Author: Bryson Smith, 9 studies

The Vision Statement
REVELATION
Author: Greg Clarke, 9 studies

Bold I Approach
PRAYER
Author: Tony Payne, 6 studies

Cash Values
MONEY
Author: Tony Payne, 5 studies

Sing for Joy
SINGING IN CHURCH
Author: Nathan Lovell, 6 studies

The Blueprint
DOCTRINE
Authors: Phillip Jensen and Tony Payne, 9 studies

Woman of God
THE BIBLE ON WOMEN
Author: Terry Blowes, 8 studies

GoThereFor.com

Have you ever found yourself in the following situations?

- Your Bible study has decided they want to start studying Ephesians... tomorrow.
- Your colleague has agreed to investigate the Bible with you, but you don't know where to start.
- You forgot to order your new Bible reading material in time.
- A family member has asked you why a good God allows suffering, and you're not sure how to answer them.

GoThereFor.com is an online library that provides you with essential ministry materials, instantly. Subscribe and download what you need, when you need it, and give your friends a digital copy (or print it for them) so they can use it with you.

No postage costs and waiting periods. No limit to the number of studies you can use. No need to clean scratches off a DVD. Just great Bible studies, personal Bible reading material, training courses, videos, ebooks, short articles and longer essays.

Visit www.gotherefor.com/join for subscription information.

Digital ideas and resources for real-life ministry

Also by Tony Payne

Fatherhood: What it is and what it's for

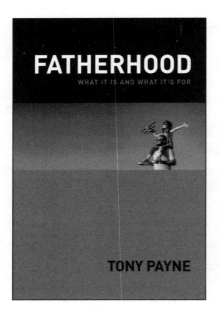

"In the course of this book, I want to change your mind about fatherhood. I want to change the way you think about it, both consciously and instinctively. And if I succeed, it will change the way you act every day in a thousand ways. It will make you a better father."

So writes Tony Payne as he takes a fresh look at what the Bible says about dads. What does it really mean to be a father? What should fathers be trying to achieve? And how can they do a better job?

Drawing on his years of experience as a father of five, Tony answers these questions with insight, practical wisdom and good humour.

If you only ever read one book on fatherhood, make it this one.

Also available as an ebook.

FOR MORE INFORMATION OR TO ORDER CONTACT:

Matthias Media (USA)
Email: sales@matthiasmedia.com
www.matthiasmedia.com

Matthias Media (USA)
Email: sales@matthiasmedia.com
www.matthiasmedia.com

Also by Tony Payne

Islam in our Backyard

An exceptional book—part novel, part essay—which goes behind the media stereotypes to examine what Islam is really about. More than this, it broaches the big questions that Islam raises for Western society: Who is God really? Is it possible to know? Can Christianity and Islam both be right? Does 'religious truth' have any place in our public culture? And even if we say it hasn't, will Islam take any notice?

Also available as an ebook.

Pure Sex

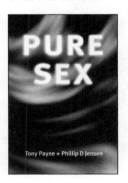

Phillip Jensen and Tony Payne take a look at what the Bible teaches about sex, and at what this means in the sexual climate of the new millennium. In doing so, they give Christians clear and compelling reasons for standing apart and being different from the world around them; but they also provide a challenge to the non-Christian person who realizes that something is very wrong with the model of sexuality we are now living with, post the sexual revolution.

PATHWAY BIBLE GUIDES

Pathway Bible Guides are simple, straightforward easy-to-read Bible studies, ideal for groups who are new to studying the Bible, or groups with limited time for study. We've designed the studies to be short and easy to use, with an uncomplicated vocabulary. At the same time, we've tried to do justice to the passages being studied, and to model good Bible-reading principles. Pathway Bible Guides are simple without being simplistic; no-nonsense without being no-content.

Available for purchase from Matthias Media or for download from **GoThereFor.com**.